The King of Waste

Written by Sascha Lawler

Illustrated by Mitch Vane

Flying Start
to Literacy®

Contents

Chapter 1

Good and bad news

When Estelle's mother came home that night, she was smiling but her eyes looked sad.

"Estelle, my dear," she said. "You know that w don't have enough food for all of us this winte The crops have failed and we are all hungry. The Queen has agreed to adopt you to help us You will live at the royal palace, where you wi be a friend for Princess Olivia."

"Oh, you're so lucky Estelle," said Sophie, her youngest sister. "You'll be living in the palace with the King and Queen. Oh, and I almost forgot Princess Olivia!"

"But we'll miss you," said Claudia, her other sister.

Every day, Claudia was hungry, like the rest of the family. There was only enough bread for everyone to have one small piece each day.

"I will miss you too," said Estelle.

"But at least with me gone, there'll be a little bit more bread for you."

Estelle knew that this day had been coming. Her mother, who worked in the royal palace for the Queen of France, had always said that if the bread ran out and there was not enough to eat, Estelle might have to leave home.

The winters had been very cold for three years now, making it hard for the farmers to grow wheat. Without enough wheat, the bakers could not make enough bread – and that's what Estelle's family survived on.

All the families in the village were hungry. And it was the same in all the villages in France.

Chapter 2

Estelle's new home

The next day, Estelle kissed her sisters and her father goodbye, and walked with her mother to the royal palace. The guard smiled at her at the grand gates, but Estelle was too nervous to notice.

They walked in through the enormous doors, up the marble staircase and down three long hallways before Estelle's mother stopped.

"This is your room, Estelle," she said.

Just then, a girl about Estelle's age stepped into the room.

"Princess Olivia," Estelle's mother said, "this is my daughter, Estelle."

"Hello, Estelle. I am so glad you are here," said the princess. "Come with me. I'll show you my room!"

"I'll see you later," said Estelle's mother. "I must attend to Her Royal Highness."

All afternoon, Estelle and Princess Olivia explored the royal palace.

That night when they were called for dinner, Princess Olivia led Estelle into the dining room. "Hello, Estelle," said the Queen. "It is lovely to have you here."

"Yes, yes," said the King, as he chewed on a turkey leg. "How wonderful to have a new guest to sample my chef's incredible creations!"

Estelle's mouth watered as she looked at the turkey leg.

"Tonight we are having creamy ham and leek soup with crunchy French bread," said the King. "It's the latest in French cooking."

Estelle's eyes lit up as the waiter placed a large bowl of soup in front of her. Although she was very hungry, she ate it slowly, appreciating every mouthful.

"What did you think, Estelle?" said the King.

"It was delicious," said Estelle. "Thank you very much for dinner, Your Majesty."

It was the first time in ages that Estelle's stomach had felt full.

The King laughed loudly, holding his huge belly. "Dinner?" he said. "My girl, this is just the first soup course!"

As he spoke, more bowls and bread were placed on the table.

"Beef and tomato broth is served," announced the waiter.

Course after course of food was served. There was an entire pheasant, large plates of vegetables, roast lamb, and to finish – three different desserts!

The King insisted that everybody at least taste each course, although Estelle could only manage a small bite of each one. The Queen and Princess Olivia also found it difficult to eat all the food.

Estelle had never seen so much food. And so much of it was not eaten.

Chapter 3

A terrible discovery

Later that night Estelle slipped quietly into the kitchen. There was something she had to know.

"Excuse me, sir," she said to the chef. "What happened to the food left over from dinner?"

"Well, some of it went to Penny and Paul," the chef told her, "and the rest is in there."

He pointed to a huge rubbish bin filled to the brim with perfectly good food.

"Oh, no," gasped Estelle. "Why did you throw it all away?"

"The King won't eat the same thing twice," said the chef. "And it won't keep fresh."

Estelle was upset, but it made her happy that at least two people got some of the food.

"Who are Penny and Paul?" she asked curiously.

"Why, they're the royal pigs," said the chef. "And they eat a royal dinner every night."

Estelle couldn't believe it. How could so much wonderful food be fed to pigs and thrown away? What a waste!

The next night after another seven-course dinner, Estelle took Princess Olivia by the hand and led her to the kitchen.

"I need to show you something," said Estelle.

She pointed to the rubbish bin, filled with roast chicken, vegetables, custard tarts and everything else that wasn't eaten at dinner. It was almost overflowing.

"Phew!" said Princess Olivia. "Why are you showing me the rubbish?"

Estelle didn't say anything. She took Princess Olivia outside and pointed to the pig pen. Penny and Paul were guzzling down roast vegetables and lapping up onion soup.

"Yuck!" said Princess Olivia. "Why are we watching the pigs? Estelle, I don't understand."

"My family is starving," said Estelle.

"They are?" said Princess Olivia.

"Yes. Nobody in my village has enough to eat. You see, the winters have been very cold and the farmers cannot grow enough wheat. And because there is not much wheat, there is hardly any bread. It's the same in many villages all over France."

Princess Olivia looked shocked.

"But what can we do, Estelle?" asked Princess Olivia. "We don't have enough food here to feed the whole of France."

"Maybe we can't feed the whole of France," said Estelle. "But we can feed my whole village with the leftover food from one royal dinner."

"That's a great idea!" said Princess Olivia. "I'll talk to the chef."

* * *

The next morning, Princess Olivia gave Estelle some fruit and bread from the kitchen, and Estelle went to her village to visit her family.

"Claudia, you look so thin," said Estelle.

"I'm okay," said Claudia, smiling weakly.

"Here, eat this," she said, handing her some bread and passing an apple to Sophie.

Estelle told her sisters about all the food at the palace and the plan that she had made with Princess Olivia.

"I'll need your help to bring everyone to the palace. Be at the gates tomorrow night just after sunset."

Her sisters nodded. "We'll be there."

Chapter 4

Let them bake bread

That night, after another enormous dinner, the King and Queen were told of a disturbance outside the gates. A guard led them outside to see what was happening.

As they reached the gates, they both gasped. There was a big group of men, women and children, and they were eating the royal food!

Some were eating hungrily and others were standing in line at a long table filled with food, waiting to be served by Estelle, Princess Olivia, the King's chef and his kitchen staff.

"What's all this?" shouted the King, suddenly angry. "Who are all these people and what are they doing at my palace? Princess Olivia!"

The villagers went silent and everyone looked at the King fearfully.

"Please Your Majesty, don't blame Princess Olivia," said Estelle, coming forward. "These people are from my village. They don't have enough bread to eat and they have been very hungry. In fact, all the villagers in France are hungry."

"All the villagers in France?" said the King. "If they need bread, they should just bake some! My chef has the most wonderful recipe – I'll make sure he gives it to them."

"But Your Majesty, they have no wheat to bake bread. And there was so much food left over from dinner that I didn't think you'd mind if we gave it to them," said Estelle.

"They are eating our scraps?" said the King.

"Yes," Estelle's father spoke up. "And they are delicious. Thank you, Your Majesty."

"Yes, thank you, thank you!" all the villagers chimed in.

The King leaned against the palace gates, looking confused, but much calmer.

Estelle led the King along the table filled with food.

"This is tonight's mushroom soup," she said. The chef was standing behind a big pot, scooping soup into bowls for the villagers.

"Ooh, that soup was divine," said the King. "But there's so much of it left."

"Yes," said Estelle. "And usually the chef throws it away or gives it to the pigs. But Your Majesty, there's nothing wrong with it. And the people from my village need food."

"Hmm," said the King.

"These are my sisters, Claudia and Sophie," said Estelle.

"Ooh, you're eating the beef stew. It's good, isn't it – the chef added some fresh herbs and a hint of spice," said the King.

"It is very nice, Your Majesty," replied Claudia. "But we are just glad to be eating something. We don't mind what it is."

Sophie nodded in agreement.

"Yes, well you do look very thin," said the King, observing Estelle's sisters. He paused for a moment, then cleared his throat.

Chapter 5

No more waste!

"I have an announcement to make," said the King loudly. "Estelle is right. This food should not be wasted. After all, it is the latest in French cooking," he said, chuckling to himself. "Chef, perhaps we should have smaller portions from now on. And villagers, if you are hungry, you may come to my kitchen each night and eat what is left over."

An excited murmur rippled through the crowd, but it was interrupted by the King's chef.

"Excuse me, Your Majesty," said the chef. "That is very generous. But the people in my village are hungry, too. What about them?"

The King looked thoughtful.

"Well," said the King, "I know wealthy lords and ladies all over France who enjoy their food ..." He paused then said, "I know, I will ask all of them to let the nearby villagers have their leftover food!"

There was a brief second of silence then a loud roar as the air was filled with the sound of the villagers' cheers.

Estelle and Princess Olivia cheered the loudest of all.

A note from the autho

I was inspired to write this book after reading about a time in France when there wasn't enough bread to eat – it was known as the bread famine. The people of France h no bread to eat while the royal family ate very well; King Louis XVI loved his food. The bread famine was one of the things that led to the French Revolution.

This piece of history reminded me of the way that food is wasted all over the world today. Many people and businesses throw out a lot of food, while other people don't have enough to eat. I think it is important that people learn not to waste food, just like the King did in this story.